Advance Praise for *Dancing at Lake Montebello*

"*Dancing at Lake Montebello* contains such moving poems, all laced with profound compassion. Viti writes beautifully about ghosts of her past, recalling them in all their full complexity and detail. By the magic of her words, she breathes life into them. Here is a writer whose poems are kindred spirits to the ones I dream of writing."

    —Julia Alvarez, author, *Afterlife*

"The more you read Lynne Viti's poems, the more aware you become how with the placement of even a single unexpected word she slyly turns her plainspoken honesty into something suddenly more intimately revealing and no less honest."

    –Lloyd Schwartz, Poet Laureate of Somerville, Massachusetts

"Lynne Viti has composed an evocative cycle of poems that become a memoir, at times tender, wry, sad, prayerful, and funny; she moves through the years of a generation that 'vowed we'd do so much better when it was our turn,' only to learn to accept that we only do the best we can—and even that is extraordinarily challenging."

    —Dominique Browning, author, *Slow Love Life*

"Viti's Charm City overflows with survivors and ghosts, yet avoids the minefields of sentiment. Snapshots from decades past—euthanasia coasters and backfin, mean girls and pheromones, talismans and to-do lists—collapse time. And "love" is in the details, the dance of the natural world, the white foam where the sandy shore and frothy water embrace. Viti has mastered the music and the moves in a collection that pierces the darkness."

    —Richard Peabody, editor, *Gargoyle Magazine*

"What you cannot know unless you hail from Viti's hometown is that on the far side of Lake Montebello is a rehab hospital by the same name. It's a place one goes to, to gain strength after something bad has happened. This collection by the Crabtown poet-in-exile offers the same."

—Rafael Alvarez, author, *The Orlo & Leini Tales*

"*Dancing at Lake Montebello* probes the profound effect memory has on an individual, and therefore all of us. In a consistently strong voice, these poems contemplate the evolution of a psyche in a rapidly changing world that includes family, race, politics, love, and friendship. Viti has a keen eye: each of her poems are imbued with salient details that reveal various intellectual and emotional effects of memory, effects that deepen and elevate our personal experiences."

—David Cappella, author, *Giacomo: A Solitaire's Opera*

"Viti's poems remind us of deep connections to family, to the tribe. With intelligence, courage and clarity the successes and failures of life become unforgettable. Loss of loved ones is acknowledged and transcended, written in poems of terrifying beauty. Here is a poet who knows the fragility at the heart of humanity—who sings her own song."

—Joan McBreen, author, *Map and Atlas*

"The poems of *Dancing at Lake Montebello* comprise the moral education of the poet, a young white girl who comes of age in Jim Crow-era Baltimore, enters adulthood in New York City in the 1960s, and looks back from the vantage of today, when so much of what the decades seemed to promise has been lost. Clear-eyed and unafraid, joyful yet elegiac, these verses treat of parents and children, lovers and friends, pinned to their particular historical moments by gesture and intellect, music and drink, flowers and styles of clothes, affirming that "though life has marred and marked us all deeply," to bear witness in words is to abide."

—Gina Maranto, author, *Quest for Perfection*

Dancing at Lake Montebello

Poems

Lynne Viti

Dancing at Lake Montebello

Poems

Lynne Viti

Apprentice
House Press
Loyola University Maryland

First Edition

Paperback ISBN: 978-1-62720-280-0
Ebook ISBN: 978-1-62720-281-7

Printed in the United States of America

Design by Catherine Tsilionis
Cover Illustration by Jeff Blum, after Herman Maril (1908-1986)
Editorial Development by Sofia Barr
Promotion plan by Sarah Conroy

Published by Apprentice House Press

Apprentice
House Press
Loyola University Maryland

Apprentice House Press
Loyola University Maryland
4501 N. Charles Street
Baltimore, MD 21210
410.617.5265
www.ApprenticeHouse.com
info@ApprenticeHouse.com

For Tom, Will and Tony

Contents

I. Girls 1

Biography 2

Parrot Jungle 3

Inheritance 4

Matinee at the Shore 7

Clifton Park 9

Labor Day 11

The Good Father 13

Hollyhocks in the Alley 15

My Father's War 16

We Called It Armistice Day 18

Lament 20

Crabbing on the Isle of Wight Bay 22

Early Morning in Highlandtown 24

My Mother on My Cousin's Wedding Day 26

Girls 28

The Color of Her Volkswagen 29

Inclined Plane, Pulley Wheel & Axle 31

Engineer 33

Dancing at Lake Montebello 35

Judgment 36

Reckoning 37

II. Love Drunk 39

At the Foghorn 40

Actor 42

Preparations 43

Nickel Dreams 45

I Can't Get No 47

Homeleaving 50

Punting 51

Starter Wedding 52

Love Drunk 54

Greenwich Mean Time... 55

Tremont Street Suppers 57

Putnam Avenue in Spring 58

Drinking Games.. 59

In Louisburgh, County Mayo, Thinking About Dublin 60

Suze in Midsummer.. 62

Brantwood Lane Miscellany 64

Pâtissière... 66

The Guitar of Solitude 68

Murphy in August 69

Ghazal: Returning 70

Shades at the Reunion 71

III. More Dangerous for All of Us............................. 73

I Learned That Marilyn Had Died.. 74

Gun Stories 76

Photos of Your Daughter's Wedding Under the Mandap,
    Not the Chuppa.. 78

Elegy for Alice, Forty-Six 80

Scattering Alice's Ashes from the Pont D'Arcôle 81

Eve's Diary 82

Sugar Pumpkins 84

Weeding the Bittersweet.. 85

Last Sunday in July 87

The Shadow of the Lost Object Falls Across the Ego 88

How You Were Before.. 89

The Dying 90

Making Love to You Was Like Peeling.. 92

More Dangerous for All of Us 93

Deep Midwinter After-Party 95

The Summer People 97

Greyhounds 99

Leukapheresis 101

Charm City 102

Leftovers 104

God's Thief 105

Walking at Day's End 107

About the Author 109

Previous Publications

A New Ulster, "Early Morning in Highlandtown," "Inclined Plane, Pulley,
Wheel & Axle," "Weeding the Bittersweet," "The Stone in Your
Chest," "Shades at the Reunion"

BlazeVox, "Reckoning," "Ghazal: Returning"

Chautauqua Review, "Matinee at the Shore"

Damfino Journal, "Gun Stories"

Foliate Oak, "Judgment," "Preparations," "I Can't Get No"

Gargoyle, "Greyhounds"

Grey Borders, "Girls," "Actor," "Dancing at Lake Montebello,"
"Homeleaving," "Elegy for Alice," "Love Drunk"

Grey Sparrow, "The Good Father," "Engineer"

Highland Park Poetry Muses Gallery, "In Louisburgh, County Mayo,
Thinking of Dublin"

In-flight Literary Magazine, "Suze in Midsummer," "The Shadow of the
Lost Object"

Irish Literary Review, "The Dying"

Journal of Applied Poetics, "Armistice Day"

Light Journal, "My Father's War," "My Mother on My Cousin's Wedding
Day"

Little Patuxent Review, "I Learned That Marilyn had Died"

Lost Sparrow: Porcupine, "Deep Midwinter After-Party"

Meat for Tea: the Valley Review, "Brantwood Lane Miscellany"

Nixes Mate Review, "Putnam Avenue in Spring"

Oddball Magazine, "Scattering Alice's Ashes from the Pont D'Arcôle"

Old Frog Pond Farm Poem of the Month, July 2016, "Last Sunday in July"

Origami Poems Project, "Hollyhocks"

Paterson Literary Review, "Pâtissière"

Pen-in-Hand, "The Color of Her Volkswagen"

Poetry Pacific, "Walking at Day's End"

Poetry Superhighway, "Biography"

63 Channels, "Making Love to You Was Like Peeling," "The Guitar of Solitude," "Punting"

Somerville Times, "At the Foghorn"

South Florida Poetry Journal, "Parrot Jungle," "Eve's Diary," "Sugar Pumpkins," "God's Thief"

Stillwater Review, "Lament"

Subterranean Blue Poetry, "Nickel Dreams"

Temenos, "More Dangerous for All of Us"

Topology, "Clifton Park"

Westerly, "Greenwich Mean Time"

Work to a Calm, "How You Were Before"

I. Girls

Biography

White girl, born in the city, grew up near the county line.
Catholic school, navy jumper, nuns in round white collars.
Negroes, only saw them when we went downtown,
on the streetcar — after North Avenue when you looked around

there were hardly any white faces. When the school day was done
the bus filled up with teenagers heading deeper into the city,
their school books stacked under their arms.
The boys gave up their seats to the girls.

I breathed the air of segregation, taking it in,
hardly knowing how it worked in this border state city
of unstated rules, takeout only, segregated pools,
separate schools, public or private, secular or parochial —

Separate movie theaters, separate stores. I graduated from saying
colored people to Negroes, still, everything stayed separate.
Brown-skinned bus drivers, trash men, busboys, day cleaning ladies.
White teachers, doctors, priests, Girl Scout leaders, hairdressers.

My black-and-white TV world:
Nat King Cole, Eartha Kitt, small figures
with big, rich voices coming from our Sylvania.
They looked so small.

That was the air we took into our lymphatic vessels,
our blood, our reproductive organs, it was our field vision.
It would be years before we'd awake (or refuse to),
to see we had not sensed a system behind the screen.

Parrot Jungle

A lizard darted up the screen.
I left my doll, half-naked, outside on the lawn.
The plastic wading pool wore inflatable yellow rings.
I wouldn't wear the bathing suit top, only the ruched shorts.

There were no children to play with.
My parents smoked and drank beer in the shade.
One night they went to the races —
I don't know who stayed with me.

We drove to a place where giant parrots in bold feathered coats
were brought to us so we'd hold them on our arms.
My mother was game —
I watched the birds perch on her pale forearms.

I stood behind my father, clung to his Miami jacket.
Pink flamingos walked around a lake.
It looked like a picture book, but larger, in motion.
My mother laughed. *Don't worry, they're tame.*

At night I lay in bed and heard the grown-ups talking,
low voices of the men punctuated by my mother's laughter.
She was with her girlhood friend, Lucille.
Tobacco smoke drifted in from where they sat outside.

The night was full of the sound of ice rattling in cocktail glasses.
My brown-skinned baby doll lay abandoned by the palm tree.
I dreamed of lizards racing across the cracked pavement
to the underside of the bungalow, cool and dark as a starless sky.

Inheritance

A fair, freckled child who knew only one person with
dark skin, hair that crinkled at the temples
with eyes the color of the rich garden earth —
might be forgiven for thinking that this woman,

who each day walked from the streetcar stop on the corner
to the child's home, half a house
spitting distance from the city-county line — should marry.
Marry was what grown-ups did, her parents, aunts, uncles —

All married. Only the priest and nuns were not.
Like the cardinals in the yard, the red male, dun-colored female,
everyone should have a partner, be one of a pair.
That child might be forgiven for foolishly suggesting

the woman who came to cook and clean should wed the man
who pushed a broom at the brick building
by the alleyway, an office building owned by a white man
the child never saw, only heard his name spoken,

Mister something-or-other, a forgettable name.
But Mister Fitcher, the handyman, was handsome.
He wore tan trousers and a white shirt.
The child's father called him Fitcher, never Mister.

When the child revealed her matchmaking plan
for Miss Burnell to marry Mister Fitcher,
her father laughed —
Fitcher was already married, had kids.

The child's imagination hadn't stretched that far,
she couldn't envision Mister Fitcher with children, a wife.
She thought he slept in the office building.
She saw him every day but Sunday

working in the alley near the back door,
always in motion, carrying boxes,
hosing down the boss's car,
hauling junk away in an old Chevy pickup.

Privilege let her grow tall,
gave her a voice people listened to.
Miss Burnell worked hard, liked her drink on a Saturday night,
had a couple girlfriends, whether drinking pals or lovers

was never clear. She worked till she was sixty-five,
The crinkly black hair turned salt-and-pepper.
The emphysema came in her later years, after the riots,
after all the houses on Biddle Street were razed.

The girl grew up, married, had a baby, sent photos to her old —
What should she call her? Who was she, besides Burnell?
Babysitter, housekeeper, nanny, minder,
the one always there after the school day ended,

when the girl burst in with her bookbag, asking
What's for supper? The one who called the mother
when the girl had a fever, or when the insurance man
or paper boy came to the door to collect the payment.

Call her by her name, Miss Brown
who came north from Virginia before the War,
who taught the girl how to iron,
how to make a piecrust,

who asked the smallest of favors,
bring that vacuum cord down here,
run upstairs and get me that dustcloth, who said
Thank you, baby, I'll dance at your wedding.

A photo of Miss Burnell Brown hangs on the wall.
She lounges, draping herself on the double bed, smiling.
Moments before the shutter blinked
she had a coughing fit.

She looks resigned, her bible and the radio nearby.
She lived another six years,
then the diabetes, the bad heart,
the emphysema carried her off.

Matinee at the Shore

At the candy store near the whitewashed movie house
we spent our nickels on cream caramels and fireballs,
stuffed the small bags of sticky sweets into our pockets.
We pulled our t-shirts down to hide the evidence.

Don't go on the Ferris wheel or the Tilt-a-Whirl,
sit downstairs at that movie house, the mothers warned,
as my older friend and I set out for Division Street.
DewAnn was a tough girl from Dundalk, sassy, full of questions.

I was three years younger, only half-listened to the mothers' rules:
Separate sections, balcony, different customs down here —
Ensconced in her booth, the ticket lady asked our ages.
DewAnn hesitated. She was tall, looked twelve —

that meant an adult ticket, fifty cents.
All but our last quarter each was gone.
We were lucky that day — the woman didn't fuss.
She tore two gray tickets off the roll, never smiled.

I followed DewAnn's long legs up the wooden staircase,
dragged my hand on rough painted wallboards as we went.
The candy bag bulged in my pocket.
Laughter met us as at the landing.

Empty seats surrounded us.
I didn't like to sit far from others
in a dark theater, even for comedies.
DewAnn said, *We can't mix.*

We'd already broken one law, no candy inside the movies.
I felt we might as well break another — but I didn't say a word.
After the newsreel, the screen turned to color.
Every soul in the balcony cheered.

But I slid down low in my seat,
stuffed another caramel into my mouth.

Clifton Park

I demanded that my mother
take me back to the park
with the three swimming pools.
Summer was hotter then.

At night fans cooled us down.
In the days we moved slowly,
drank iced tea or Kool-Aid.
I asked her to take me to the city park

with the three pools, concrete-bottomed, concrete-sided.
The baby pool, the pool for grown-ups
the middle one just right for me.
I waded cautiously into the shallow end,

watched boys dive into my pool,
swim like fish through cold water.
Their skin was dark,
their hair in dark little whorls in perfect patterns.

I pestered my mother to take me back.
She shook her head. *Why,* I asked. *Why not?*
All summer I contemplated the three pools, the boys
calling out challenges to one another,

shoving, laughing, scrambling
onto the pool's concrete edges.
Why, I kept asking — *Why*
don't we go back there?

Polio, she answered.
And too many city people.
I understood polio
but the rest confused me.

What could be better than
to be near those boys, their skin shiny,
their shouts, name-calling, bragging
in our pool, in our city?

Labor Day

It was a day out, a day off.
They stocked the boat with bait and tackle,
Luckies and Camels, sandwiches and beer,
headed for where the bay meets the ocean.

There were plenty of stripers in those days,
bonitas, perch when your luck ran out,
more blues than you could catch and clean,
supper and then some, all glistening prizes.

To say something went wrong that day
is to turn away from the sun on their faces,
the sun on gray water,
beer cans they drained, tossed overboard.

To say something went wrong
is to ignore the yells when one of them
startled out of half-sleep.
The boat stopped drifting, dashed against the bridge.

I can't say if there was silence or moans
as they made way to shore,
to City Hospital's green corridors,
to black telephones to call home.

My father dragged that leg around for years—
that natural prosthesis, ankle fused to foot.
He was early to bed then.
His arsenal of pills filled the bathroom shelf.

One day he taught me to hit a softball
directed my stance, placed my hands on the bat,
warned me never to daydream at the plate.

The Good Father

The good father fell asleep on Saturdays
stretched out long on the couch.
Or he hoisted me onto his shoulders
or carried me into the ocean,
keeping a firm grip on me
which was fine by me.

The good father took me to church
let me play with my white prayer book
with the gold cross hidden in a place inside the cover.
He pointed to the altar in front
when the three bells rang —
the priest held the white circle bread high.

The good father slept in the big bed
on white sheets with blue lines.
He lay next to my mother, slender, dark-eyed.
Laughter came from their room at night.

He drove us to Florida in his gray car with three pedals.
I tried to stand up in the back all the way to Virginia.
Dirty water came out of the hotel's faucet in Charleston.
We heard the trains whistle all night.

He brought me a Charlie McCarthy doll
so I could talk to everyone and not be so shy.
He brought me a doll so I could rock her
even though she was not my child.

He smelled of aftershave and orange bath soap.
I traced the scar on his forehead with my small hand.
And later, the sad father came to our house.
He wore a heavy brace on his leg.

A black steel bar ran up the side of the boot.
He walked with a wooden cane.
Bottles of pills filled the medicine chest.
He was early to bed — we had to be quiet then.

Hollyhocks in the Alley

A flower from an English cottage garden,
a word hard to wrap the tongue around,
a six-foot-tall stalk with colored orbs, one maroon
so dark it fades into licorice black.

We stood on our godmother's wooden porch
looking towards the alley that ran alongside her yard.
In narrow garden beds that lined the concrete walkways
tomatoes prospered in the city heat.

We watched the hollyhocks, tall as men.
They loomed week after week
as each bright green bud awaited its turn
to open into a flower with a five-inch span.

We tracked their progress,
counted bees that poked into those flowers.
They weren't staked — we never saw anyone
stand over them with a watering can.

They took care of themselves till September
when their spent blossoms hardened
into fat seed pods stuffed with black disks.

My Father's War

He'd always loved boats, being on the water.
Enlisted in the Navy at thirty-three, took up smoking too,
signed up for top secret hazardous duty overseas.

But he didn't go to sea — he went to
fight Japan from the ground in Manchuria,
aerographer's mate first class. He told us he

learned to track clouds — cirrus, cumulus, nimbus. Shaved his
head, all the men did, naval intelligence said
that would fool the Japs when they flew over.

They lived with Chinese soldiers and spies,
ate rice and whatever meat
their hosts could scare up. It might have been dogs.

I forecasted the weather, he told us, but
the records say otherwise: to Calcutta for indoctrination,
how to eat with chopsticks, never insult the Chinese hosts.

Flew over the Hump, on to Happy Valley, east of Chungking.
Lived in camphor wood houses, drank boiled water.
History books say they spied on Japanese ships,

blew up enemy supply depots, laid mines in harbors,
trained Chinese soldiers in guerrilla warfare,
rescued downed aviators.

When he left for San Pedro, my mother saw him pack
a long knife and a gun in his suitcase.
Orders, he told her. *Top secret.*

He told the same story twice
about the gash on his forehead that
grew fainter till it was a thin line

etched on his weather-beaten brow.
He returned from his war malnourished, his teeth
rotting, he drank whiskey, chased it with beer.

He brought home silks embroidered by the Maryknolls.
He hated the Communists, Chiang Kai-Shek was his man.
I never knew it till after he died —

he was no weatherman.

We Called It Armistice Day

Until we didn't—on parents' day at school
our teacher asked *Does anyone know*
the new name of this day —

I turned around, looked at
my father seated on a folding chair
leaning against his cane —

cracked, speckled terrazzo floors
in the halls, dark wood in the classrooms.
Windows climbed up to the ceiling.

Playground, half-cement, the rest blacktop —
the farther from the school, the rougher the boys played —
the girls sat on the brick wall by Christopher Avenue,

in sixth grade some got bras, the rest of us were
flat-chested under our white safety patrol belts —
My father always asked, *Was her father in the service?*

Army? Navy, maybe? Only my uncle stayed out of the war
— he was too old, had kids had asthma —
My father got a scar on his forehead

and a smoking habit, lost forty pounds in China.
He claimed he studied the clouds in Manchuria,
ate rice and — he averred — dogs and cats,

flew over the Hump — then sailed to Oran,
took a troop ship home, limped off the gangplank.
My mother said he didn't sleep well,

her Dalmatian growled at him.
My father didn't like the house
she'd bought when he was away —

He bought the Legion's paper poppies after church
or in the Food Fair parking lot.
I kept them on my dresser clear up till Christmas.

Lament

I dreamed my father was the ocean —
salt water lapping, reclaiming the beaches —

or he was Poseidon, with his trident, ruling the seas.
Only my father didn't rule the water.

The salt waters of the bay and the booze
conspired to push the boat on which he dozed,

sunburned, sated with whiskey. He was slammed
against the pilings of a small bridge. He never

walked right again. His football days were long
over. Now he couldn't show me

how to run for yardage after catching the pass.
He couldn't drive a standard because his ankle

screamed when he depressed the clutch.
From then on it was automatic Chevys for him,

all the way, power steering, too. He graduated
from crutches to brace and a cane from Mexico,

a green snake curling up the wood
swallowing the tail of a black snake.

There were no ramps in those days, no special
parking places, no seats in the aisle, no elevators at

the stadium. In the car window, he held up his cane,
called *Hey, Mac! Can I get a good spot up front?*

When I walk along the beach, tide on its way in,
winds propelling the water under my feet,

waves so high no one dares wade in,
I know my father was never the sea,

was never king of the sea,
but a toy of the churning water.

Crabbing on the Isle of Wight Bay

At an old footbridge we set up —
Tied the chunks of eel to twine, threw the lines
as far as we could, so the crabs
might think they'd chanced on a choice breakfast.

Pull the lines gently, my father said, *draw*
the string in slow and steady. We stayed for hours,
not much to do but test the lines, nibble sandwiches
a half at a time, drink grape soda from the can.

We gazed down at the current.
The lines made parallel cuts in the water.
Throw him back, my father instructed
when we netted a small one.

Too, there was his prohibition
against keeping the female,
her apron marked by deep ridges.
I turned the net inside out and let her go.

That night in the cottage kitchen
we splashed beer and vinegar into the pot.
Barehanded, my father lifted the scuttling creatures
one by one from the cooler, dropped them into the pot.

We sprinkled the crabs with Old Bay.
I heard them moving about, rattling against one another,
then it was eerily quiet. The sweet, spicy smell
of crab suffused the room.

I breathed it in deeply.
We hammered away and picked,
praised backfin and clawmeat,
licked the seasoning from our lips.

Early Morning in Highlandtown

In my mind's eye I see it — the stub of a macadam road
dead-ending into Blue Diamond Coal, its trucks

lined up each morning for the long hauls.
To the left, the junkyard, heaps of metal and rubber,

hard by an Italianate house, rust-brown, coated with years
of dust and cinder ash, facing the junkyard cranes.

A porch swing, always vacant even on summer
evenings. Only the metal cranes saw.

The folks who lived in the house, white-haired, plainly dressed,
bespectacled, came and went together, but mostly stayed home.

My father's tavern sat amongst these places, the last
in a row of houses. In its former life, the bar

housed a bakery, we heard — the baker's family
lived upstairs in the cramped rooms, their kitchen

the bakery itself. I used to pretend I could smell
bread baking, the sweet fragrance of airy

white loaves turning golden in the long-gone ovens.
I went along with my father there before dawn,

the half-light bathing the block in a sepia glow.
I sat at a small table in the back bar reading comics —

or on the ragged sidewalk I stood peering down
as my father slid each beer keg into a hand truck,

rolled it up a plywood ramp, and into the tavern.
Light crept in through the glass bricks in the storefront.

I leaned around the corner of the darkwood bar,
watched him roll the keg from handcart to its station,

waited for the hiss when he tapped the silver barrel.
I inhaled the faint yeasty smell, which oddly, offended —

and pleased me. Sounds of traffic began to flow in
from the bar's back door, propped open. I was

sent to pick up the paper from the doorstep, laid it
on my father's worktable near the jukebox.

It wouldn't be switched on till lunchtime.
Hank Williams' and Jerry Lee's wails would issue from it.

But by then I would be back home — quiet streets,
small green lawns — lolling on an old quilt spread in shade.

My Mother on My Cousin's Wedding Day

Children weren't invited. That
wasn't fair. I was thirteen,
had never seen a wedding, except on television.
She opened a flat box of stockings,
pulled them on gently, fastened them to her girdle.
I watched her pull the beige lace dress over her head,

shake it down her slender frame,
gently push her arms through the sleeves.
I zipped the dress closed.
I climbed onto her bed, mesmerized by the lace sheath.
Paid full price too, she said. Coral high heeled pumps,
matching handbag, sparkling costume jewelry.

She leaned towards the mirror to put on her lipstick,
coral, like the shoes. From a department store box
she withdrew an ivory hat, broad brimmed in the front,
covered with perfectly matching ivory tulle.
My father waited downstairs in his favorite chair
trying not to sweat in the August heat.

I followed them out the front door, sat
on the porch steps, the concrete hot on my thighs.
The green and white fins of our Chevy disappeared
down our street of identical brick houses.
She was forty-five. I knew
she'd be the prettiest, best dressed lady there.

She wore the lace dress over and over, and the coral shoes.
But the hat stayed in the back of the closet for years
till one day the square box went to Goodwill
because nobody wore hats anymore.

Girls

We never sensed privilege in the air we breathed.
We thought if life wasn't fair, at least

our parents, our teachers were. The President was.
We believed all men were equal, women too —

We thought the woman who came five days out of seven
to do our wash, clean bathrooms, cook our meals

was like family — we never asked why she never married,
lived downtown in a cramped apartment we visited only once.

I saw a wide Windsor rocking chair that used to be ours,
a bed from Sears our family gave her.

I peered out the living room window to
the movie theater across the street, its name — *The Roosevelt* —

in orange neon lights. A colored theater, we called it. I saw
the front wall of yellow bricks, flakes of paint dotting the sidewalk.

She took the city bus, we rode in a car or a taxi.
Nights, when heat stalled over the harbor, suffused the city,

our Chevrolet glided through neighborhoods of people on stoops,
fanning themselves, drinking iced tea from glasses robed in condensation.

Mothers watched over shirtless boys dancing by the hydrants,
the cold city water shooting onto black asphalt.

The Color of Her Volkswagen

Atlas blue. First Bug I ever saw.
It showed up one day, a shiny little thing
in Miss Kay's driveway two doors down,
their old Dodge long gone.

People on our street drove Chevys or Fords,
nobody even knew how to say Volkswagen,
were skeptical about a foreign car, but Miss Kay
packed up picnic basket, playpen, her kids, suntan oil,

squeezed us all into the Bug.
I watched Miss Kay shift the gears, her pedicured feet
depressing the gas pedal, working the clutch
like an extension of her body. She tuned

the radio to WFBR, the Four Lads sang
Standin' on the Corner Watchin' All the Girls.
When we got to the swimming place, an old
quarry now flooded with water, now a club

where you bought a daily membership,
the loudspeaker blasted my kind of music —
There Goes My Baby — repeated every hour.
We ate peanut butter sandwiches,

Miss Kay plunged into the water from a dock.
She wore a green bikini, adjusted the top
over her breasts when she surfaced.
I rubbed her suntan oil on my arms and legs.

Around us, older girls mixed iodine and baby oil,
greased up their arms and legs and shoulders,
lit Newports and blew smoke rings.
I longed to be like them.

Homeward, the VW rolled up and down country roads
back to the city, steaming streets, dried little lawns.

Inclined Plane, Pulley Wheel & Axle

for Mary Jane

I studied the euthanasia coaster,
the Lithuanian artist's drawings, the steep
first stage of the steel thing, the sharp
drop meant to cause hypoxia to the brain,
seven inversion loops, clothoids
designed to drive passengers into brain death.

At the end of the ride, wrote the artist, they'd unload —
unload! —the bodies, then do it again with fresh comers.
Strange to think that coasters that thrilled generations
of those four feet or taller who climbed into the toboggans for fun,
could be made into death machines, for euphoric and elegant death —
to solve the problems of life extension.

We rode the old wooden coaster once.
When the bar was secured we gripped it hard,
shrieked and screamed, which made it
all the more wonderful. My hair
blew behind me and my stomach
leaped up into my heart, which jumped into my throat.

Your father came to the front door
for his weekly visit, his old car
parked in front of your house.
We were off to Gwynn Oak Park with him —
your brother, you, and I. Did we ride
the Deep Dipper or the Little?

I dreaded both, but you promised
your father would sit between us.
We'd be tucked in safe and we could
yell as loud as we liked.
The ascent scared me far more than
the fast drops towards earth.

I hated the creaking of the toboggan train as it
made its way to the crest.
But the plummeting was a joy, we curved around a bend
and it started again, the slow climb.
Three times I felt pure bliss,
heard a scream shoot out of my head.

Your father was solid between us,
he laughed and hooted. It was
the only time I ever saw him happy.
You were a brave girl.
I was uncertain about roller coasters.
You stayed in Baltimore, married, had kids.

I left as fast as I could and kept moving.
You died before you were fifty, leaving me
to reconstruct my memories.
You wouldn't like this Lithuanian artist's notion,
his good-death coaster,
the trip through euphoria to quick death.

Hearing him, you'd tug at your blond hair, turn,
walk into the sunny afternoon
far from the black toboggans.

Engineer

He loved trains of all kinds, and trolleys —
back when they ran along the roads to Carney and Towson,
all the way to the route's end, Woodlawn or Windsor Hills
places I knew only as names on placards, black print on white

in the front of those streetcars or white on black
on the turning signage at the side of the car,
Irvington, Forest Park, each mysterious terminus.
He set up the Lionel trains on the sheet of plywood

painted green to look like fields, trains that ran past a station, a school,
a town hall, fields with tiny metal cows that grazed on painted wood.
He wore the motorman's hat or the engineer's striped cap,
stacked glossy train magazines on his bookshelf,

talked about steam locomotives, electric trains, straw-seated trolleys,
bus routes through Baltimore till his world expanded and he learned
the subway lines in New York and Boston, discontinued private
companies,
public utilities, anything so long as there were cars carrying people

or empty cars late at night or in the first run out of the car barn.
Car barn — when was the last time someone used those words?
Now he's often confused, often unsure of how to log into email,
uncertain which day it is or where his wife goes when she leaves the
house.

The cops came one day, he might've done something wrong.
They pushed him down into the squad car as he yelled,

Talk to my wife, please, call my wife, she'll explain.
It's nothing like that, we later heard.
It's his mind, it's slipping, he fears he can't remember things —
won't remember the stops on the Number 19 line
won't remember where they built the diesel-powered buses
their fumes sweet and nauseating all at once.

When we were young he let me start the train,
drop a pellet into the engine's smokestack.
Gray smoke, pungent like incense, poured
out of the engine as it clicked along the tracks.

Sometimes he let me throw the switch
so the train turned off onto a loop that led
to the roundtable where he did repairs, touched
up the paint, let the engine rest.

Heads together, we leaned over the platform, the tracks
in the train world he created.
Light slanted in through the basement window.
Look, he said, flicking on the red signal.

He slowed the train to a halt, pointed
to the coal car. *We need more fuel.*
He threw the switch then. I thought
he was king of the railroads.

Dancing at Lake Montebello

The road at night was ours.
We sang happy birthday to you, who cajoled us
to dance around the edges of the reservoir
in the headlights of our parked car at midnight.

Friday nights we glued ourselves
to the sofa in your family's den.
You explained who Oscar Levant was,
why we should be amused by his patter.

We heard Monk play jazz in a black box theater.
You steered us to the best Chinese food in town.
You schooled us, this is how we first saw the world
splayed open before us, for us.

Judgment

Two nights after
the president was shot
my mother went out.

She put on silver blue eyeshadow.
She wore her Persian lamb jacket
with the mink collar.

It was the year
she was having the kitchen redone.
The house was in disarray.

I sat on our brocade sofa.
I watched the small black and white TV.
It sat in a temporary place atop an end table.

I watched the news replay
Jack Ruby shooting Oswald.
A boy I thought I liked came by.

I didn't like the way
he chugged from the green Coke bottle,
swished it around like mouthwash before he swallowed.

I never forgave my mother.
I wanted her to sit
on the sofa with me and cry.

Reckoning

Out of her basket of recriminations
She pulls the same one as before —
thoughtless adolescent girls, we spurned her, made sure
she couldn't enter our circle. We spun
invisible walls around ourselves at lunch,
in the hallways after school, at the bus stop.

Decades have stacked up — we've grayed, our worn bodies
have spread or require discipline to stay within old boundaries.
Our feet suffer from bunions, or perhaps a hammertoe.
We prefer elastic waistbands, we might walk
with a cane, or favor one leg or hip, not quite
a limp, but a listing, now and then.

She spies me across the banquet hall —
a hundred women between us —
takes me to task for the third time in thirty years.
It's always an embarrassment, knowing I —
who fit in only by luck, the stars,
the charity of girls who like me

adored the Beatles, Chinese food,
Steve Allen's antics — was the object
of anyone's envy. We locked her out.
I utter a bromide: *Adolescent girls
can be so insensitive*. This doesn't
mollify — the grievances aren't done.

I listen, nod, my eyes darting in search of rescue.
I do not say what I know for sure:
I'd do it all again if I had the chance, fly to those girls,
throw up barriers against the others.

We five circled around one another for a year before we coalesced —
Beatles Forever, Thelonius Monk, Mee Jun Low on a Saturday night.

II. Love Drunk

At the Foghorn

for Sam Cornish

Tall awkward boy, a transplant from Oregon,
always carried a beat-up paperback of *On the Road,*
straphanging on the #3 bus
asks *You like poetry?*

He tells me *go hear this cat read his stuff.*
Black dude, he's real, man, get there
before the show, he goes on before the folksingers,
down on 22nd Street, you dig?

I roll my eyes at this farm kid from the west
who thinks he's cool, but I take note:
The Foghorn, I check the listings in *The Evening Sun,*
below the flicks, above the Gayety Burlesque ad.

I tell my mother I'm going to a poetry reading,
as if in a college lecture hall, on a school night.
I'm the youngest there. People sit around drinking beer.

A young man, bespectacled, dressed in brown corduroys,
crewneck sweater, steps onto the stage.
Cheers and foot-stomping greet him — he's here to be heard
by the faithful. He recites his poems, declaims them.

I've never heard a poet, not in real life — the nuns
have played records of Dylan Thomas, of Eliot
in English class but nothing like this, a real
poet, not a dead white one — standing so near

I could shake his hand — he is mesmerizing,
he looks at us through thick eyeglasses,
he speaks in the vernacular.
I came for the poetry, and when he was done

I went home to make curfew. I didn't
come for the guitars and banjos,
The mandolins and Woody Guthrie tunes
— I came for the poetry.

Actor

When we met on the steps outside Levering Hall in winter,
he told me his favorite song was Greensleeves,

his cigarette Marlboro, the writer he adored most, James Joyce,
and did I want to see him in *Le Balcon* next weekend, because

he had the role of Chief of Police, and afterwards we could go
to the cast party at Fred and Charlie's flat but I was seventeen,

still in high school, my parents would never have gone for it,
so I declined but not before I accepted a cigarette and a light

saying *maybe next summer when I turn eighteen.*

Preparations

Don't kid yourself
into thinking that the past isn't still
stuck fast inside you, no matter how you will it
away or meditate until you think you touch

infinity, or the edges of it, if infinity
has edges, like the edges
of the yellow walls where they met
or the edges of the wooden window frames

in the room where you gladly gave up
your virginity, another thing
on your to-do list before college.
That longhaired girl with ivory skin

freckled in summer, body slimmed
by regimen of hardboiled eggs and grapefruit
— she's still with you. She stretched out
on the narrow bed, raised her arms

above her head, looked into the eyes
of her novice lover, the one
she chose for the deflowering,
as if she might find some clue,

some notion of how to be a woman.
And after, when the thing was done,
she was done with him as well.
It was more or less a disappointment,

an act to have behind her.
When he left that day, she knew
that one more line
could be crossed off her list.

The old steamer trunk her aunt had lent her
sat in the hallway,
its drawers and shelves
waiting to be filled.

Nickel Dreams

Along the Fuller Brook path wending
through backyards, there's no one about
except a few women with small dogs on leashes.

The brook not as high as I expected,
blackened piles of snow all melted,
roof rakes, ergonomic shovels, the chemicals

strewn on sidewalks and porches, mere memories of winter.
The sun strains to appear.
It warms the day but I can hardly

see my shadow, or perhaps faint
suggestions of a shadow, a darkening, barely perceptible.
On a day like this, full of spring's promise,

I cut an armful of jonquils from my mother's garden
wrapped them carefully in newspaper, a cone
around the yellow blooms so fragile their stems could easily snap.

Go to 30th Street Station, Mike advised, *for the transfer*
but watch out if you're there right at six, when
the dogs are let off their leashes,

dogs in gray flannel suits, carrying
smart leather briefcases. I understood. He loved
to quote Dylan: *Don't sing in the rat race choir.*

As I rose near my stop on the Paoli local
an old man glanced at my flowers.
I withdrew one and handed it to him,

without a word, hopped off at Haverford.
Mike stood on the platform, his long scarf
artfully draped around his neck, tweed sport coat festooned

with buttons of Lenin, Freedom Now, Stokely Carmichael.
We walked through his campus,
his arm around my shoulder.

This will be my life, I thought.
His roommates were out. We
skipped dinner, built a fire. We

talked about the war, about Yeats.
When it was late and we were so hungry we couldn't stand it,
we strolled to the Blue Comet for cheeseburgers —

I remember even now how good they tasted.
We took the back way to the women's college
— I'd set up camp in the guest lounge.

Mike kissed my cheek, handed me a nickel
the Paoli local had flattened into an oval,
Washington's head all distorted.

I carried it around for years,
that talisman of my life to come.

I Can't Get No

for MWM

Satisfaction, we danced in the basement to the Stones.
Your mother introduced us to her boyfriend.
They sat upstairs drinking iced tea.

The August night was humid,
The lightning bugs were already out dancing
across the wide lawns.

You'd survived a year of college.
I'd slimmed down, to prepare for it.
I grew my hair long,

pinned it up into a French chignon
trying to look like a girl in a Truffaut flick.
You were the only one who noticed.

No satisfaction, no satisfaction.
You danced with everyone at your party
Beach Boys or Stones or Smokey Robinson —

You kept your hair short, close
to your head. You still favored the
madras shirts, khaki pants, boat shoes, no socks,

you were the preppiest guy I knew.
I never saw anyone who
could dance like you, with such abandon.

It could be Mersey sound, blues beat, r&b.
You were an equal opportunity
Music loving dance machine —

At midnight when I knew I had
to collect my girlfriend and get home
though I wanted to stay and dance with you

I threw my arms around you
turned my cheek so my ear
was up against your clavicle.

You were breathless, smelling of
Lark cigarettes and soap
Call me tomorrow, you said.

I walked up the stairs to your mother's kitchen
I drove across the city in my father's Chevy
to my part of town.

My hair had come unpinned.
I slipped into my nightgown,
washed my face. I felt so lucky

you were my friend, one who asked so little,
who made me laugh and shared
his cigarettes and his Scotch with me

his fake cynicism and his jokes.
You were never my boyfriend,
never my lover. You were

the companion who years later left a poem
rolled into my old typewriter,
blue-black ink, corrasable bond.

Homeleaving

Driving north from Baltimore, we found the turnpike empty.
Maria's mother had a heavy foot on the gas.

It's been decades since I loaded that station wagon
with my clock radio, winter clothes, the green Smith-Corona.

I traveled light — half a dozen books, my Brownie camera.
We reached Tenafly by midnight, its tree-lined, unfamiliar streets.

I unpacked, fiddled with the radio, searching for music to wake up to,
lay in bed thinking of what I didn't yet know I missed —

The brick rowhouse's small rooms, shallow closets.
The soft sound the morning paper made when it hit the porch.

Tomorrow I'd make my way to the city — bus from the corner,
subway from Port Authority to Morningside Heights,

the college's black and gold iron gates flung open,
odd new faces, strange smells, under the same blue sky.

Punting

Elvis had just died in Memphis — he was forty-two.
You and I'd just moved in together
to a third-floor walkup in Brookline.
We were just in Cambridge for a couple of days,

long enough to rent a punt,
travel up the River Cam for just a few lazy hours.
I lay back in the boat while you pushed the pole,
I read you the King's obit from the *Herald-Tribune*.

Just the two of us on a calm Tuesday,
drifting, then and later, back home,
for a short while, not quite in love,
just close, a stepping stone

was what we had, just enough for then,
a short prelude to our separate lives.
Now a fragment of that day comes back:

your boyish laugh, your golden curls
glinting in the English sun.

Starter Wedding

I had the wedding I wanted—no white gown.
I chose a Vogue pattern, the dressmaker sewed it
of blue crepe, shoes dyed to match, I wore
tiny silk flowers tucked into my hair —

The best man said I looked like Liz Taylor
— we were standing in the mist at the side door
of the Cathedral of Mary Our Queen.
At the very moment my betrothed and I stood at the altar,

Jackie Kennedy was marrying Aristotle Onassis on Skorpios.
We all know how that turned out, not
exactly a love match. My father wanted
a nuptial Mass, Ave Maria sung by a soprano

me kneeling before the statute of the Blessed Virgin,
laying my bouquet at her feet. But I was marrying
a lapsed Baptist — so no Mass, no Blessed Mother —
and I wanted to toss my bouquet at the reception.

The priest was brief, uttered the necessary words
to constitute the sacrament of matrimony —
my uncle was scandalized by my minidress.
My mother had handwritten the invitations, short notice,

everyone though I was pregnant.
I cried when my aunt embraced me,
handed me a tissue, whispered, *Don't ruin your makeup,*
you'll look like a raccoon.

My groom wore a bespoke suit. Slender,
at twenty-four his hairline already receding,
he was beaming, it was the happiest I ever saw him
that day, when it all seemed so promising.

Jackie Kennedy and me — brides with different motives.
If you'd asked each of us six months later,
we might've agreed on this much —
some people get married for the wrong reason.

Love Drunk

We made our vows in the lady chapel.
The reception was in my family's house,
fifty of us crammed into the small rooms I grew up in.

We drank too much champagne — the Veuve Clicquot you chose.
My mother whispered to us it was time to leave
for our weekend honeymoon at your brother's cottage in the valley.

I threw my bouquet from the top of the staircase.
Your brother's girlfriend caught it —
I wonder if she knew all along he was gay.

We slept on cotton sheets he had dyed red on the stove.
Our life together faltered, then frayed.
It seemed so long while we lived it.

My memory's blurry, vague, with necessary omissions.
Except I remember the tart, crisp champagne,
our rich wedding cake, devil's food iced with buttercream,

the cool sheets on our first marriage bed,
waking up and staring into your ice-blue eyes,
knowing we couldn't turn off that road we'd set out on.

Greenwich Mean Time

In a time of a war halfway across the world —
a war we didn't want, one spurred by old men,
we fled the city, taking our books and music,
our marriage bed and secondhand table.

In my grandmother's station wagon
up the Henry Hudson Parkway we rattled along
into Westchester, onto the Merritt,
everything we owned we'd stuck in boxes or pillowcases.

We settled into a rented flat over a garage.
The kitchen's four windows admitted the morning light.
We eschewed meat, discovered tofu, kasha, spinach noodles.
We dined on garbanzo beans and cashew butter.

Our paychecks covered rent and gas, groceries,
food for the cats we brought home from the pound,
a calico and a black one who sucked his paw when he dozed.
We drove very slowly down Cat Rock Road in snow.

The city seemed so distant. The birds that stayed
all winter darted from one naked tree branch to the next.
Weekends, we lay in bed till ten, reading the paper,
nestled against each other under an emerald green spread.

You hadn't found work yet. In December you sold
Christmas trees from a Port Chester lot, freezing your hands,
so used to office work, the telephone and the foolscap pads.
Our idyll became worn at the edges, there were quarrels

over nothing, over money. We sold the motorcycle
to pay the oil bill. We missed the museums, the subway,
the long walks from midtown to home, the news kiosks,
the confectionery with chocolate enrobed Florentines.

We missed the faces of people we passed on the street,
Everyone in suburbia was white, with perfect teeth.
Everyone seemed happy with the way things were going,
in the town, in the country, in the broken world.

Tremont Street Suppers

Nixon was President. We didn't yet see how
to get rid of him. He was bombing Cambodia.
We tuned in nightly to the war summary on WBAI.
The men acquired draft deferments —

One of them, blind in one eye. Another saw
a psychoanalyst twice weekly, his parents paid.
Our friends hadn't married.
There was always flirting, assignations

where young people found themselves — the library,
the nature museum north of town, the diner,
the natural foods store with the prototype electric cars
lined up in the parking lot, waiting for the future.

We met for frugal potlucks, the appetizer a shared joint,
the main course a vegetarian concoction
from a counterculture cookbook — dessert was
a bowl of ice cream with a half dozen spoons stuck into

the decanted mess, or almonds we dragged across
a saucer of honey before leaning back to savor
the evening's music — we wanted the evening to last
longer than the workday, wanted love, wanted romance.

You and I wanted to be made for each other —
the others circled around us, patchouli-scented distractions
we did not see for the danger they were to us,
to our fragile tandem state.

Putnam Avenue in Spring

Overnight, melting snow gave way to waves of daffodils
covering the hill near the Protestant church.
But churches hung in our peripheral vision,
an annoyance, a reminder of what we'd cast off.
The public library was our church, the holy source where
we plunked down a ten-dollar deposit, carried home
projector and cans of classic films spooled on reels.
On a sheet tacked on our living room wall we gazed
at sepia images of the Little Tramp sauntering down the street
swinging his cane, smiling shyly at the girl of his dreams.
Scott Joplin rags hummed on our stereo, background sound.
We stretched out on the rug, throw pillows under our heads.
Too tired from the workday, too stoned to make love,
like orphaned siblings, a family unto ourselves.

Drinking Games

At dinner I drank too much cheap red wine,
free carafes of it served with the steak and potatoes.
I was a mean drunk, carried on about a piano
I insisted you buy for me — I snapped my eyeglasses in two

in a teary display — I loved those tortoise frames.
A few weeks later I got sloshed at a party, I'd gone alone —
you never liked the Unitarian crowd.
They drank scotch before the meal, wine with dinner,

brandy after dessert. I've never been so sick —
retching in the bathroom till nothing was left
to come up, I slumped over the basin, holding a cold cloth
to my forehead. All the next day I ate nothing

but crushed ice, cursed myself, wondered
how I'd gotten home at all, did I say
anything rude or off-color or
vomit in the powder room before the party ended?

There was something I couldn't grab hold of,
a thing that had taken hold of me. I only drank
with friends or people I wanted as friends.
I drank to be someone I wasn't.

It was worse to do nothing.

In Louisburgh, County Mayo, Thinking About Dublin

The smell of burning peat in this steady morning rain
suggests a memory out of reach, something from years ago

when I got the notion to drain my small savings account,
head for Ireland, once final exams were read, grades in,

textbooks collected, counted, accounted for, our bosses
satisfied that the City of Stamford had gotten its due.

I was twenty-six, marriage in shreds, divorce papers drawn up —
I was seeking a different self, a poetic self.

I stayed a week in Dublin, wandering the streets Joyce describes.
Each day I distracted myself from the hole in my life,

went to the Abbey, met an American actor, a minor
figure on the Broadway stage who took me to an after-hours place

frequented by the Dublin theater crowd — I could've sworn
when we knocked and the actor whispered the password,

the man who peeked out and opened the door was Milo O'Shea —
The actor and I drank Jameson neat, sipped it slowly.

In Boyle, County Roscommon, town of my great grandmother,
I wandered the cemetery, searching for the Sheekey graves.

The headstones from the days of the Great Hunger hid in the high grass.
I rented a small red Ford, drove across Ireland,

slowing down, braking often for the sheep, accepting waves
from old farmers as I shifted into first gear, on to the next village

stopping each night to find a room and perhaps supper —
supper identical to breakfast, eggs and rashers,

brown bread and white, tomato, tea, lashings of butter —
I ate too much and drank the Guinness, which fattened me up —

I outsized my waistbands. I was growing in my grief.
Instead of wasting away, I came home a stone heavier,

a bottle of Jameson in my duty-free bag.

Suze in Midsummer

Not exactly a beauty but you couldn't take your eyes off her.
Dark hair, clear skin tanned year-round, eyes lined with kohl.
She favored caftans or empire waist frocks.

Her narrow feet were encased in Greek sandals,
her golden arms ringed with bangles.
Husky-voiced, with an easy laugh, she drew to her

every man in sight. When one of them won her
for a month or two, the rest stepped back,
petitioned to be her friends, to stay in that golden orbit.

I used to be heavier, she confessed, but
I owe this — she gestured from slender
neck to painted toenails — to wine,

beer, coffee and — she held
up a tightly rolled joint, slid it
between her lips, accepted a light.

She played a field of unattached males, then
settled into domesticity, Upper West Side style,
moved in with a New York radio DJ, honey-voiced

like her, only in a deeper register.
She acted off-Broadway, knew where
theater people supped late nights, wove macramé.

Maybe she married the radio guy, lived
happily or not, as so many of us who
married and divorced, not knowing the odds.

I could probably find her now — it's so
easy with the Internet — unless someone wants to
erase herself from the databases, change her name,

win no prizes, publish nothing, refuse to embrace
social media — unless she is not a daughter who
survives her parent, or a sibling —

unless she becomes a non-person online, even if a
somebody to neighbors, coworkers, children,
maybe even grandchildren who point to photos

in leather-bound albums, asking Glammy, who's
the lady with the dark hair and the bracelets sitting
in the lounge chair, holding the tall frosty glass?

Let me be clear: I don't want to
find Suze, only want to remember that
night at someone's parents' Connecticut house

when they were away. We commandeered the
kitchen, concocted vegetarian salads, opened beers,
bottles of Chianti. She watched the men watching her.

I saw it all, her pheromones, her pull on us,
her laughter spilling from her to us, overflowing porches,
running loose down suburban streets.

Brantwood Lane Miscellany

August to August, we made a little family.
The house was too big for us.
That year there was always a confluence of menses.

A stream of lovers, either too young or too old
sent by well-intentioned matchmakers
passed through the door. None stayed long.

We were barely women then, more like girls:
One insomniac, one hard of hearing,
one itching to go north.

We came and went by the front door
turned away the Jehovah's Witnesses
shutting the door hard, laughing nervously.

At night we sipped scotch or shared a joint.
Mornings, two of us drank coffee,
one wouldn't touch the stuff.

I cooked, Martha did the washing up.
Our mascara stained the white towels.
Our laughter annoyed the neighborhood.

When we left for good
the garden was just bearing fruit.
We missed out on that harvest.

Workdays, the morning all-news station
poured from the upstairs bedroom,

sometimes I was startled out of sleep at 3 a.m.
by twin noises, the vacuum and the stereo.

Pâtissière

The December you made a poundcake
your mother's fat cookbooks were stacked in the white kitchen.

The cupboards were so high you had to stand on a wobbly stepladder.
I steadied it as you pulled down the old china from Sauveterre.

It was painted with tiny roses and vines.
Plates just large enough for a fat slice of buttery cake, dotted

with gold raisins and crushed pecans.
You couldn't have been more than fifteen.

That winter you made your way through
Craig Claiborne, James Beard, Julia Child.

I'd see you chin resting in an open hand, one elbow
on the white table, the other flipping through stained pages.

That egg yolk yellow cake was just the moister side of dry
but not dry, so solid I could make a meal of it. *Have another,*

you told me, slicing through the thin brown top
into the golden mass of cake.

A pound of butter, a pound of flour,
a pound of extra fine sugar —a recipe that's almost not a recipe at all.

You went off to college, immersed yourself in semiotics,
found a boyfriend, then later, a husband, a divorce,

a business partner, then two. You got
a love, a child, a flat pictured in the *Times* Home section.

There have been awards all these years
but not for cakes. There have been

honors, attestations, prizes. You're famous,
on panels, on juries, you're in Wikipedia!

Has there been no poundcake? No chipped china
from your grandmère? No recipe that's not a recipe at all?

You wore small tortoise shell glasses,
your hair needed a good cut.

You wiped your buttery hands on your flannel shirt
scraped the last bit of batter from the bowl.

You wrapped dish towels around your hands,
slid the cast-iron pan into the oven.

Come back in two hours, you said,
we'll have cake for dinner tonight.

The Guitar of Solitude

The guitar of solitude leans on the bookshelf,
its strings loose. It's out of tune.
Blond wood, near-perfect fingerboard.

It calls to me, mostly in the evening
after a Lenten supper of soup and bread,
no wine. Water with lemon, or weak tea —

The guitar says *turn these knobs, make*
my strings taut again, press your
fingers against my wires, start

with something simple like "Where
Have All the Flowers Gone," *move on*
to rock and roll, play a riff from

"Smoke on the Water" *or* "Whole Lotta Love, "
come on baby, rock me
all night long, won't you?

But there's laundry,
bill-paying, taking out compost,
a race to the end of the day

chores, flossing, baby aspirin, set
the alarm. The guitar leans back
rakishly. Maybe tomorrow.

Murphy in August

Those without air conditioning in the dog days of summer
found cold shelter in the neighborhood movie houses.
On such a night we collected you from the bus station.
Fresh from your years in Freiburg — long-haired, bearded,
last off the bus, you schlepped a backpack and your guitar,
came for one last party before we had to grow up.
By the time you came down to Baltimore,
we were cutting our hair, dressing for success.
You were the last to dip your toe into adulthood,
trade your busker's license for a programmer's desk.
That humid night the 'Sixties were over,
the 'Seventies half gone. The moving sidewalk
didn't care who was left behind. You hopped on —
to a job, marriage, two kids, and a 401(k).

Ghazal: Returning

Can I go back there, can I return today,
by happy accident of physics, fly there today?

Transport myself back to those pale rooms,
those hallways full of laughing girls, today?

We leaned in doorways in late afternoons,
confided secrets, triumphs, as we might today.

Our hair was gold, chestnut or raven, catching light
from sunlight's slant through windows, like today

but stronger rays, intense, in memory's eye.
We sang in empty classrooms, looking towards today.

Who were we then, and are we still the same —
though life has marred and marked us all deeply — today?

Thread the way back through the long tunnel of years,
with young girls' eyes see who we are today,

Make time collapse, forgive the petty sins and slurs
we have committed, reconcile today,

Recall when all was bright before us, all was fresh,
vows not yet made or kept or broken, as today.

Memories of youth infuse this hour —
yesterday, the future, evade our reach — we grasp today.

Shades at the Reunion

When we gather like this around the table,
every five or ten years, drinks in hand, raising toasts,
in the back of our minds, always, are the ghosts:
the cousin who died at forty, when the cancer flared.

The school friend, gone at barely fifty — she loved her smokes.
Toxins and her genes did her in.
The rest of us — we've survived,
though we're not sure why or how.

My friend the hard-edged newsman
laughed when he told me his on-air transition phrase —
"elsewhere in the news"— as if we could
move from tsunami to oil spill to death of an ex-president

with any kind of grace. When he lay dying
in his hospital bed in Croton-on-Hudson
this old journalist stared at TV images of Baltimore burning.
It's all like it was before, he murmured.

Knowing all this, we sit in the cool air,
September sun on our faces,
hearing the songbirds carry on
like Yeats' miracles in Byzantium.

III. More Dangerous for All of Us

I Learned That Marilyn Had Died

Not Monroe but Marilyn the English teacher
who befriended me the first day of my first job
who invited me to her thirtieth birthday —

the inveterate New Yorker from West Virginia
who lived in a tiny studio on the Upper East Side
when nobody could afford to live there.

Marilyn who taught me how to sew pantsuits
when it was radical to wear them to school.
Who had pale skin and black hair

a long face, a cutting word,
who wouldn't let her students say, *This is boring*,
but made them say instead, *This did not reach me*.

Marilyn who slept with my ex after our breakup —
(he can't remember this because
he never remembers anything he did before
the new millennium).

I lost touch with Marilyn after she met a man
on the train coming back from Lake George.
She called to tell me she was engaged,
warned me not to get involved with a younger man.

I ignored her, never saw her again.
She liked dogs, a special breed, I don't recall which one.
She never married, became one of those beloved teachers
everyone remembers forever —

Her father used to leave her and her kid brother
locked in the car on his way home, he stopped at a bar,
he'd be in there for hours drinking —

I'd never heard of a Jewish alcoholic or Jews in West Virginia.
She said they weren't observant,
never went to temple, there was no bat mitzvah.

She loved the theater, the students, the Upper East Side,
expensive scotch, fine restaurants in midtown, and the beach.
She loved Gatsby, Hamlet, Sylvia Plath, Melville,
Anne Sexton, John Donne.

She had the saddest face even when she smiled, and
black lashes against white skin.
Her dark wit made me laugh and wonder
really, what was so funny about what

was so sad. I wish I knew
what became of her, before
her short ticket was punched.

Gun Stories

Outside the house the suitors line up,
a long queue of them, starting at dawn.
Each one with a gun.
I can see them from my bedroom window
— their handguns in holsters,
or rifles slung over their shoulders

like lawmen in my father's TV westerns.
In town, the fire chief shot
his brains out with his service weapon.
It happened in his official car behind
the fire station on the main street.

I lost a friend over the guns her son
brought back from the army,
along with a crumpled marital history
and a taste for oxy.

Once a black Luger was interposed
between me and the hand that held it.
It was pointed at my father's head, and then at mine.
The hand swept the gaze of the gun across the room.

Now the women have armed themselves, too.
Paper targets, then miscreants, then
intruders at the city gates
overflowing into exurbia, the neighbors' dogs —

those go first, felled by your bullets.
When there's no one left to shoot, your gun might be turned on you.
I know if I got my hands on one I'd drop this embroidery,
sneak out the back door, go looking for a blacksmith.

I'd apprentice myself, I'd want
nothing more than to hold the black gun
over the fire, pummel it.
— You'd thank me for this.

Photos of Your Daughter's Wedding Under the Mandap, Not the Chuppa

On a night many nights after we spent
five days a week in a fluorescent-bulb-lit classroom
you made grilled salmon with pesto,
sweet roots roasted in your silver oven.

You poured the Beaujolais,
I hovered my hand over the glass
to slow you. We killed two bottles.

Talk of decades ago, I was young,
you were younger, our words danced around the years,
wove stories of those you knew and I didn't
or ones I knew and you didn't, or
boys and girls, now grandparents, we both knew —

In the morning I saw photos of your daughter's Indian wedding —
bridesmaids with hennaed hands and arms,
each arm extended as they danced,
the groom and bride weighed down
under their rich wedding garments, their crowns.

You saw to it that a branch of cypress from your yard
was tucked with the flowers pinned on orange cloth.
You'd tended the plant for a chuppa someday —
now it graced the mandap. Your husband
tried to look comfortable in turn-up khussas, long white kurta.

We could've talked all day but I had a train to catch.
All the time I rode back to Boston
ignoring announcements, next stop New Haven, Kingston,
things were happening — unfolding, the media reported,
in California. Long guns, body armor, shooters,
They came prepared, the police chief told reporters —

So many dead, trapped in offices, watching,
so many questions, theories, posts online.
Rifles and handguns, holiday banquet,
police chase, shootout—we've seen this movie before.

Ammo rounds, remote control toy car, explosive device.
Thumb drives, cellphones, car rental agreement.
The AG said, *This is not what we stand for,*
this is not what we live for.

Prove to me she is right. Show me we live for
the wedding day, sunny November, pale bride,
dark groom under the mandap,
the grandmother in a bright blue shawl.

A day of peace, utter joy under bright Connecticut sky
— what we live for, who we are.

Elegy for Alice, Forty-Six

Your brain bled out on one side, then the other,
sent faint messages to your lungs —
orders that grew fainter, like a fading telegraph
in a sinking vessel on a distant sea,
emitting weak dots and dashes
till all went silent.

Your brothers, their wives, your sister and your mother,
your children sat in Adirondack chairs
on the green lawn of your new house
the one you worked so hard to paint,
to get the feng shui perfect —
Tree branches formed a heart against the sky.

Your work was looking at the stage, describing
every detail the sighted noticed.
We asked who'd now explain to the blind
what the actors were doing when
they entered a living room or stood atop a mountain
to sing a paean to the American experiment, or to a beloved.

Last year you admired my magenta shirt
the one that caused hummingbirds to dive-bomb me
when I wore it in the garden on August mornings.
I wish I'd given it to you on the spot, so you could've
drawn the hummingbirds too, watched their beating wings
in the fleeting, full-flowered garden.

Scattering Alice's Ashes from the Pont D'Arcôle

I.

Sunlight dances on the Ziploc bag.
You tear it all the way open, tip it.
Half of our share of Alice's remains
tumbles into the green Seine —

We watch the rippling water move from bank to opposite bank.
The ashes join detritus as the river routes itself to the sea,
holy remains and flotsam married in the dark waters.

II.

When you shake the plastic pouch,
the greater part of its contents,
are lifted, borne by the wind into the Paris air.

We see Alice's spirit knows a trick —
moves in water, yet it rises,
her fiery essence mutates into light and motion.
What's left of her is distilled into perfection.

III.

We cross to the Quai des Fleurs, marvel
at the top-heavy hyacinths, fat tulips.
Alice would've loved
the impermanence of this day.

Eve's Diary

The garden was there before we were. It was
so easy to tend. We had only to pluck

the ripe fruits, gather flowers — I loved the red ones best —
to fashion garlands for our hair. Mine

was long, I combed it with my fingers,
pulled it hard to one side, always to the left —

braided it so that the rope of golden hair
grazed my shoulder, fell over my breast.

We sometimes pruned branches
after the deutzia dropped its last white blooms,

tossed the clippings in the corner of our vast
yard, returned to lie under the rose-covered pergola.

We spent our days singing, entwining our limbs,
lying heart to heart, devised word puzzles.

That was before the gypsy caterpillars stripped
our trees, left their dry casings on bare branches.

The crawling things pupated,
emerged as anxious, dust-brown moths.

That was before my misstep, my foolish infatuation,
the thing that at first seemed so innocent —

a little conversation each morning
over the fence, with our neighbor.

He was a lithe creature, mysterious,
his reserve eroding each day as we chatted about

the perfect roses, ever-blooming hydrangeas,
sky-blue delphiniums — he, too, was a lover of gardens.

My story was plastered everywhere,
My shame — and my man's — became a tale you all

told to your children, a moral lesson —
our eviction was a trope, a meme.

None of you forgave, had a shred of empathy.
The landlord — we never met him — sent his constable,

a long-haired fellow with a gun in his boot,
to throw us out. He locked the gates.

Nowadays we live in what some might call a hovel.
I scratch the dry earth with a stick, trying to grow food.

The best I can do is lamb's quarters, plantain,
bitter greens for salads, or bait to draw a single bee or butterfly.

At least we two stayed together,
huddling together in the long winter nights,

wishing to forget those golden days,
shed the memory of home.

Sugar Pumpkins

We grew them in raised beds, their vines profuse, orange fruit scant.
Hard to grow *Cucurbita pepo* in a drought season.
Still, the six we found shading themselves under their companion leaves
made us think we'd grown enough to feed ourselves all autumn long.

The orange globes sat on the mantel for months, past Thanksgiving,
when we exiled them to the foyer to make room
for Christmas rosemary and holly branches.

Tonight, we choose the largest sugar pumpkin,
carve a hole in the top, scrape out the seeds and strings.
In goes the mixture — rice, grapes, walnuts, onion,
enough cumin to give it some heat.

When it's baked to a turn, we slice it from the center,
so slender arcs of pumpkin fall into a circle, looking
more like a flower than a squash. It tastes of pie
and of curry, redolent of the summer earth.

Weeding the Bittersweet

Sneaked in from Australia or Asia, settling
wherever it could, not minding poor soil,
rocks, sand, clay. Conquered woodland and garden.

We used to love the bright orange berries
popping from their yellow shells.
We used to cut it at the roadside.

Across her dashboard
one of my housemates
strewed the stuff, the berries

dried out and rolled around, fell into our laps.
We'd find crisp yellow bits in our sweaters.
We didn't know it would take over, strangling

the sacred blueberry bushes along country lanes,
digging deep into maple saplings. So insidious,
this woody invader, and overnight — or was

it decades? — claimed territory, and more again.
Today, I'd had enough.
Armed with clippers, gloves,

twine and saw,
I pulled, dug, cut, separating
harmless branch from berry-laden twigs,

pulled up the stuff by the roots,
yanked it down from struggling small trees
freed blueberry shrubs

invited bearberry and young oaks in freed-up space.
Tomorrow, for this interloper, it's the trash.
You fooled us into thinking your orange-and-yellow

was harmless, was innocent.
We twisted your vines into November wreaths,
hung them on doors,

brightened our winter tables
against nights that arrived early in our march
towards the shortest day.

Last Sunday in July

Sun, then not-sun, clouds.
Then not-clouds.
Warm, then not-warm.

This slender land can't make up
its meteorological mind today.

Cool breezes,
fungi of every color erupting —
red, colonies of chocolate brown
or white and innocent-looking,
something you might find in your salad.

Not much to do save
listen to Bill Evans ply the piano
wrestle with the crossword.

Turn off the phone. Dream.

The Shadow of the Lost Object Falls Across the Ego

A faint image, so vague you hardly know
if what you miss so much was there to begin with.
Other times, what once seemed so present
sucks the breath away, you gasp for air —

but only for a second. You don't die, not yet —
that's a long way off, though at this moment there's
darkness, the tight grip on the belly, the dank sheets,
the narrow bed traded for the old accommodating one.

This wave of absence edges out hunger and the need
to stand under the pelting water
of the morning shower.
Nothing is as it should be, or as it was.

Freud, who got almost nothing right,
explained it: The ego bends under the weight of loss,
flattened, wanting to sink into stink and hunger.
This is all insupportable.

You take a decision,
climb out of your sweat-soaked bed,
plod down wooden stairs in slippers,
pretend there's something to get up for,

if only a nod from the man who every trash day
combs the overflowing barrels.

How You Were Before

Stage 4, primary site lungs,
in late photos, in a wig or with wisps of your own hair —
not the frizzy mass around your face when
I first met you, a sunny day, East Cambridge

houses compressed against each other, backyards
of pavement or patch of grass.
Always lean, you grew thinner — ungrew —
your brown eyes more piercing than ever.

If I could talk with you now I would ask what it's like —
are you conscious of consciousness,
if the dark's kinder than the cold light
or the morphine rush that eases pain but slows the heart.

We sat on a stoop and joked while
The rest carried out moving boxes,
pushed them into the rental truck.
Your long legs in shorts were so graceful,

brown from the sun, strong enough to carry you
through your thousands of days ahead.

The Dying

They're so inconsiderate, waiting to let go of this life
on the cusp of Christmas and Boxing Day

Thanksgiving, some holiday or other,
or a cruise up the Pacific coast.

We wait and we watch the dying
in their brave decline.

They smile at the nurses, keeping up appearances.
They pretend to want to stick around awhile longer.

So long do we expect their ends to come,
so many times they cry wolf, we start to think they're immortal.

So we plan the Christmas feast,
bake the cakes, spread the damask tablecloth.

We pour the wine, tell ourselves
we might as well keep on as usual.

We pull on our best gloves, brace against the winter night
to ballet or symphony or slide into an old coat

amble down to the corner tap for a beer
and the hockey game on the widescreen.

All the while the dying carry out their plans,
wait to slip away when we're out of the room

or when we nod off in hard chairs at their bedsides.
They take their leave when we're on the road at dawn,

driving fast so we can be there to witness
their last rasping breath.

The dying complicate things for us.
They care only for dying,

have forgotten what we need or want from them.
The dying have one last job to do, alone.

They do not want our views on the matter.
The dying will die when they are good and ready.

Making Love to You Was Like Peeling

Making love to you was like peeling
an onion. I teared up, holding the knife's edge
against paper-thin layers, pulled them
away, one by one by one. I knew I must
get to the tender parts of you, underneath.

It was like scraping the hairy root vegetables,
carrots, pale parsnips, the knife blade flat
against the tubers — I needed strong hands
to hold you, to interlace my fingers with yours
to show you how desperate I was.

At night, after sex, I should have been exhausted
but I heard you turn on the shower, call
to me to join you. Afterward, I enfolded you in
a rose-colored towel big enough for two.

It was like rinsing tender lettuces in the sink,
wrapping them in cloth to dry.

More Dangerous for All of Us

In the night we're awakened by a strange whine,
loud enough to hear through the bedroom window
open just a crack to let in fresh air as we sleep.

But whether the sound's emitted from the predator
or its dying, eviscerated prey, we can't say.
A bobcat, maybe — they've turned up lately
moving east every year, arriving here, close to the sea.

In the morning, after coffee, the newspaper,
after checking email, performing the requisite stretches
to keep back, limbs, fingers and toes functioning,

I slip outside in my bathrobe and clogs, search
along the garden wall seeking evidence, scan the dirt
for clues of a crime, a hawk descending on a squirrel,

a coyote carrying off a wayward vole that
forgot to stay beneath the snow.
I find nothing, no clue of violence.

Inside, our small cat is safe. She stands
at the French doors that look out to the deck,
and beyond, to the yard, that wilderness she'll never
explore at dusk, or in the wee hours.

Life is more dangerous now, I tell her.
For all of us but especially for you,
my mackerel tabby friend,

whose prey is plastic or cloth, whose claws are clipped,
whose ears are perfect, unmarred silken jewels.

Deep Midwinter After-Party

Empty kitchen. Morning of snow. Small birds
make quick round trips from bush to feeder.
Hardly a sign of the knot of guests who last night

stood by the back doors, beers in hand
or gathered at the table of empty plates,
glasses half full of wine.

Traces of crackers and salsa marinate
with vegetable peels in the compost tub.
We used to be busy with kids and pets,

used to be the ones driving south for Christmas
or rushing home to pay the babysitter,
wondering if we'd ever make up lost sleep.

I saw you lean back in the yellow armchair
listening to the thirty-year-olds
talk about work, their children, the news.

It made me wonder at how time
had moved up so fast, how
we ignored it as long as we could.

We don't have time for forty years to reform the country,
we barely have time to read the books we want to,
plant the gardens,

see refugees welcomed, resettled,
find a possibility of peace on the planet, home to our
benighted race, drowning in stuff or in our confusion.

Years ago, thinking about this didn't faze me.
We would make it better, we would stop a war,
we would bring down a sneaky, lying President.

We vowed we'd do so much better when it was our turn.
Soon we'll march, show what we stand for, bear witness.
I'm not yet ready to call it quits, but close.

Let younger people take the reins. I'm
straggling at the back of the crowd as it pulses down
Independence Avenue. You might glimpse me there,

like the gray panthers I used to see on the picket lines
—when I was young and fecund—
time biting at their aching heels.

The Summer People

Near Uncle Tim's bridge stands a dwarf tree with twisted branches
tiny white blossoms about to fall — white sand,
shells of horseshoe crabs, not as many
as in years past. Matted salt hay, soft underfoot.

Across the marsh, the old cannery-turned-yoga studio
by the fish shack, empty parking lot,
freshly paved with crushed oyster shells,
bleached, pristine, waiting for the summer people.

In winter they stay in their houses, reading the paper.
Some sit at the piano, plunk out a few tunes.
They write letters to the editor, eschewing email,
preferring paper, envelope, self-adhesive stamps.

They walk their letters to the mailbox,
wait for the metal clank as the missives
disappear into the blue container
— pickup, 4 p.m.

The summer people in winter wear
their good coats to the opera,
don sports gear for the hockey games.
They go to work early, they're the last to leave the office.

They stand for O Say Can You See and O Canada.
They lug their groceries in reusable bags.
They watch the calendar, dreaming of the marsh,
the kettle ponds' clear water, the warm waves

late August afternoons on the bay beach,
shell-cluttered sand near the rock jetty
a fat orange sun
slow dancing down to the horizon.

Greyhounds

Our Uber driver says we don't look like bus people.
Here at the depot, in a tangle of shopping center roads

are families, a man in a wheelchair, in a row along the wall.
We get tags for the suitcases, hug our backpacks close.

Ticketholders clutch their belongings, balancing them in their laps.
Cell phones, Walmart bags stuffed with veggie sticks, nacho chips.

The station smells of something unidentifiable, maybe
stale food, matted hair, layers of clothes that need laundering.

Those with nothing but time and twenty-seven bucks
take the bus from Austin to Laredo, an all-day affair.

We join the snaking line, inch our way to the man in the DayGlo vest.
Too old to be working, he stows our gear in the belly of the bus.

Inside, the bus smells like the station — worn, sweat-infused.
We slide into two vacant seats, watch the parade of passengers.

The driver paces the aisle, speaking English first, then Spanish.
He shouts the rules: *No alcohol, no smoking, no drugs*.

It's not Simon & Garfunkel, we've not gone to look for America,
we only wanted to see the Alamo and the missions.

We ride with the survivors whose teeth and skin show everything.
They're bus people every day of their lives, they pay cash.

We keep our well-worn credit cards and wallets
hidden in the front pockets of our jeans.

Leukapheresis

For Don

There's a dispute in your blood,
red cells against the white.
You're in no shape to talk.

We're playing your music,
it fills the living room.
You're having another procedure —

it spills out unpronounceable names.
They're taking the white cells
from your blood. Let them.

Leukocytes, they're taking you into custody
so the capillaries can do their job, submit
to collection, centrifugation, spinning.

The basophils (Greek, *basis*, base, *philein*, to love),
the polymorphonuclear leukocytes,
those feisty granular immune cells,

the eosinophils, who so love *eosins*, the acid dyes,
that they embrace the stain, must be silent.
The rest of us, here at home this February day,

do what we can. We wait.
Wait, from Old French, *guaiter*,
wait and watch over.

Charm City

Downtown disappeared as we packed up our childhood things,
went to college, resisted the pull of home,
succumbed to the scent of independence.
We didn't know about birth control, weren't ready for sex,

spent hours gazing at fashion photos of formal dresses
for proms — or military balls at the southern men's schools.
We borrowed long white gloves, clutch bags, fake pearls,
monitored our alcohol intake, fended off advances,

watched foreign films with subtitles, learned to roll joints.
Uptown, we practiced our driving, took our road tests.
City buses were for others — we were meant for better things.
Downtown, the department stores packed up, moved to the suburbs.

The posh steakhouses grew tired and empty, as their patrons
died off, grew too old to travel, began to lose their teeth.
The shoppers' favorite drugstore closed the counter service,
where we lunched on tuna sandwiches, chips on the side.

The management avoided sit-ins by agitators from the campuses,
undergrads of different races in pressed chinos and V-neck sweaters.
Secretaries and file clerks tottering in heels across cobblestones,
over trolley tracks, leather bags in hand, once ubiquitous,

disembarking from city buses each morning —
vanished almost overnight, along with the appellation "Miss."
The boy we celebrated because he could drink a case of beer
— and not pass out — was drafted into the 5th Infantry, C Company,

died in Quang Tri Province, the memory of his round face,
his Beatle haircut so faint now — we traced his name on the Wall.
Downtown, the cranes went to work making a shiny marketplace
in the footprint of the old harbor. The spice factory migrated

to the county, dispersed cinnamon air among cul-de-sacs.
Shops and rowhouses burned, were abandoned, boarded up.
Then the hometown football team sneaked out of town at midnight,
the moving vans heading west to the city of Indians.

Leftovers

The cat keeps watch by the window, stares at a sunless day.
Her head turns, ears on alert, when two juncos alight on the deck.
The Christmas tree's colored lights look garish in the morning.
Half-drunk bottles of Cabernet litter the kitchen counter,
red carnations in the table settings have gone limp.
Please don't ask about the children, no longer children, now men,
back at their own digs. We haven't heard from them
since they packed up their gifts and the leftovers in plastic tubs.
They could be sleeping all day, or filling out job applications,
or heaving weights at the gym, might be watching YouTube,
how to cook favorite foods of *The Wire*. Any hope of grandchildren
on the horizon is misguided, don't ask about that, either.
Extreme climate: eight degrees at eight a.m. The President
won't stop tweeting. I watch the juncos, brave against the cold.

God's Thief

God sees me carry the stones from the seashore, smooth
gray rocks I cradle two at a time, pulling them close

to my belly, carrying them like the physical therapist said to.
If it's against the law to carry these rocks home

to my garden, well then, I'm God's thief.
God sees me snap off the forsythia branches, try

to speed up spring, make sunlight and water
push out small green leaves, butter-yellow blooms.

They brighten my spartan workroom.
God sees me out among the weeds and the damp spring soil

when I should be writing.
God knows the faces of our friends are drawn tight

in those last days before their bodies give out, their souls
still burning hard and bright in our memories.

If only God weren't so silent, so distant with us,
if only God would pull up a chair, act like

a parent imparting advice, say *When I was your age,
Rome wasn't built in a day, keep your friends close* —

I've gathered so many rocks now, each time wondering
when God will show God's self, or give me a sign —

not a miracle exactly, but a perfect rose, then another,
a summer of roses, safe behind a wall of sea-smoothed rocks.

Walking at Day's End

Explain to me how the sea puts parentheses around the years
since my father held my waist,
we jumped the waves, and he sang off-key to me.

So much time has stacked up — I walk along at low tide,
the water here dotted with bits of red seaweed,
feel only the water and the sand,

walk over shells of small crabs, or parts of their legs,
till the sea laps up again and there is only
foam at the water's edges.

Show me why the sea is so much like
old words on the page,
why I can read and reread a poem

its meaning constant
text embedded deep in my neurons
though life whirls me

from single to married,
childless to primagravida to mother of two
to mother of two grown, off in the world.

About the Author

Lynne Viti, the daughter of a Highlandtown tavern owner and a schoolteacher, was born and raised in Baltimore, Maryland. She is a senior lecturer emerita in the Writing Program at Wellesley College. A graduate of Mercy High School in Baltimore, she attended the College of Notre Dame of Maryland (now Notre Dame University), and received her B.A. in English from Barnard College and her M.A. from Teachers College, Columbia University. She earned her Ph.D. in English and J.D. from Boston College, where she was a university fellow. She has also taught at several other colleges and universities, including Boston University, Boston College, Olin College of Engineering, and Brandeis University.

Viti is the author of two poetry collections, *Baltimore Girls* (2017) and *The Glamorganshire Bible* (2018), and a short fiction collection, *Going Too Fast* (2020). Her poetry, nonfiction and fiction have appeared in over 150 journals and anthologies, including T*he Wire: Urban Decay and American Television, The Baltimore Sun, Welcome to the Neighborhood, Bad Hombres & Nasty Women*, and *Callinectes Sapidus*. She has been awarded recognition in the WOMR/Joe Gouveia Outermost Poetry Contest, the Allen Ginsberg Poetry Contest and the Glimmer Train Short Fiction Contest, and has been nominated for the Best of the Net Anthology and the Mass Book Award.

Lynne Viti lives in Massachusetts with her family.

LYNNEVITI.WORDPRESS.COM
TWITTER: @LYNNEVITI
INSTAGRAM: lynne_viti

Apprentice
House Press
Loyola University Maryland

Apprentice House is the country's only campus-based, student-staffed book publishing company. Directed by professors and industry professionals, it is a nonprofit activity of the Communication Department at Loyola University Maryland.

Using state-of-the-art technology and an experiential learning model of education, Apprentice House publishes books in untraditional ways. This dual responsibility as publishers and educators creates an unprecedented collaborative environment among faculty and students, while teaching tomorrow's editors, designers, and marketers.

Outside of class, progress on book projects is carried forth by the AH Book Publishing Club, a co-curricular campus organization supported by Loyola University Maryland's Office of Student Activities.

Eclectic and provocative, Apprentice House titles intend to entertain as well as spark dialogue on a variety of topics. Financial contributions to sustain the press's work are welcomed. Contributions are tax deductible to the fullest extent allowed by the IRS.

To learn more about Apprentice House books or to obtain submission guidelines, please visit www.apprenticehouse.com.

Apprentice House
Communication Department
Loyola University Maryland
4501 N. Charles Street
Baltimore, MD 21210
Ph: 410-617-5265
info@apprenticehouse.com
www.apprenticehouse.com